Pulling Down
𝕾𝖙𝖗𝖔𝖓𝖌𝖍𝖔𝖑𝖉𝖘

Achieving Spiritual Victory through Strategic Offense

Henry M. Morris III

INSTITUTE
for CREATION
RESEARCH
Dallas, Texas
www.icr.org

Dr. Henry Morris III holds four earned degrees, including a D.Min. from Luther Rice Seminary and the Presidents and Key Executives MBA from Pepperdine University. A former college professor, administrator, business executive, and senior pastor, Dr. Morris is an articulate and passionate speaker frequently invited to address church congregations, college assemblies, and national conferences. The eldest son of ICR's founder, Dr. Morris has served for many years in conference and writing ministry. His love for the Word of God and passion for Christian maturity, coupled with God's gift of teaching, has given Dr. Morris a broad and effective ministry over the years. He has authored numerous articles and books, including *The Big Three: Major Events that Changed History Forever, Exploring the Evidence for Creation,* and *5 Reasons to Believe in Recent Creation.*

PULLING DOWN STRONGHOLDS
Achieving Spiritual Victory through Strategic Offense
by Henry M. Morris III, D.Min.

First printing: January 2010

ISBN: 978-1-935587-01-9

Please visit our website for other books and resources: www.icr.org

Printed in the United States of America.

TABLE OF CONTENTS

Some statesmen and generals try to avoid the decisive battle.
History has destroyed this illusion.
— Karl von Clausewitz[1]

During His earthly ministry, Jesus declared that "the gates of hell" would not prevail against His church (Matthew 16:18). This imagery does not depict merely a defensive posture on the part of Christ's church, but rather a strong, ongoing attack by the Church against those "gates" of hell—eventually rendering those gates impotent. The apostle Paul wrote that Christ is the victorious Head of the church (Ephesians 5:23; Colossians 1:18), and His many commands to church leaders have never intimated that we should simply strive to survive until He returns.

GOD REQUIRES ACTIVE WARFARE AGAINST WICKEDNESS

The first and most important rule to observe...is to use our entire forces
with the utmost energy. The second rule is to concentrate our power
as much as possible against that section where the chief blows are
to be delivered and to incur disadvantages elsewhere, so that
our chances of success may increase at the decisive point.
— Karl Von Clausewitz

Consider these instructions from the Lord:

The "Last Days" would be filled with a litany of evil men and evil philosophies (2 Timothy 3:1-5).

1   The quotations from Karl von Clausewitz were all taken from his 1832 classic, *Von Krieg* (On War). The 1928 English translation initiated by James John Graham and Frederic Natuesh Maude was published by Kegan Paul, Trench, Trubner & Co., Dryden House, Gerrard Street W, London, England. The Clausewitz book has been updated and reprinted in the United States by Oxford University Press, New York.

- "Scoffers" would deny the historicity of the creation, the global Flood, and the supernatural preservation of the present world (2 Peter 3:3-7).
- Some would leave the faith for "seducing spirits and doctrines of devils" (1 Timothy 4:1).
- Even though we are to be faithful to "preach the word," there will be those who will "turn away their ears from the truth" and be "turned unto fables" (2 Timothy 4:4).

However, in spite of this worldwide and all-pervasive wicked environment, we are commanded:

- Pray and expect "thy will to be done in earth as it is in heaven" (Matthew 6:10).
- "Teach all nations…to observe all things whatsoever I have commanded you" (Matthew 28:19-20).
- To "open their eyes, and to turn them from darkness to light, and from the power of Satan unto God" (Acts 26:18).
- Within the Church, the "pastors and teachers" are to edify the saints, ensuring "the unity of the faith, and of the knowledge of the Son of God, unto a perfect man, unto the measure of the stature of the fulness of Christ" (Ephesians 4:13-14).

Therefore, the ongoing mission of the Church is portrayed as a spiritual battle.

- We are told to "war a good warfare" (1 Timothy 1:18).
- We are commanded "to be strong in the Lord" and to "put on the whole armour of God" (Ephesians 6:10-11).
- We must be fully armed, because "we wrestle not against flesh and blood, but against principalities, against powers, against the rulers of the darkness of this world, against spiritual wickedness in high places" (Ephesians 6:12).

Thankfully, even though we must "endure hardness as a good soldier of Jesus Christ" (2 Timothy 2:3), we are promised:

- We can resist the devil, as we are "steadfast in the faith," even though he is like a "roaring lion" (1 Peter 5:8-9).

- The devil will flee when we resist him (James 4:7).

- God has supplied sufficient supernatural weapons that are "mighty through God to the pulling down of strong holds; casting down imaginations, and every high thing that exalteth itself against the knowledge of God, and bringing into captivity every thought to the obedience of Christ" (2 Corinthians 10:4-5).

The World Is Going to Hell

The first, the supreme, the most far-reaching act of judgment that the statesman and commander have to make is to establish...the kind of war on which they are embarking.

— Karl von Clausewitz

The vast majority of the world's population is blithely jamming the "broad way" that leads directly into hell (Matthew 7:13). One does not have to be a widely-read scholar to recognize that the whole world is "groaning and travailing in pain" (Romans 8:22)—and it seems to be getting worse. Western society is growing more sensual and secular. Movies and TV productions are more aggressively wicked. Evolutionary humanism is overtly promoted in every conceivable venue and media.

Atheists have become emboldened and virulently anti-Christian, illustrated by the deluge of atheistic books in the past few years (Amazon lists over 2,000) with such titles as *The God Delusion* by Richard Dawkins, *God Is Not Great* by Christopher Hitchens, and the ever-present *Atheist's Bible*. The "in" thing in academia, as well in political and media circles, seems to be promoting atheism and disdaining Christianity.

The banner headline on one of the more famous atheist websites reads "The Atheistic Revolution." Early in 2009, a brash advertisement appeared on the sides of 800 London buses, declaring, "There's probably no God. Now stop worrying and enjoy your life." In the United States, the Coalition of Reason later placed billboards in key cities across the country that read, "If you don't believe in God, you are not alone." The New York Coalition of Reason paid for billboards throughout the New York subway system that touted the slogan: "A million New Yorkers are good without God. Are you?"

You might ask, "What's that have to do with me?" May I suggest that the message being broadcast by these groups is alarming in its vitriol and intensity, and should be sounding a clarion call to the Christian community that the enemy's battle against the truth of God is both startlingly real and focused directly at those who would "earnestly contend for the faith which was once delivered unto the saints" (Jude 1:3).

THE CHURCH'S BATTLE PLAN

The best form of defense is attack.
— Karl von Clausewitz

The ancient city of Corinth was a seat of intellectualism in its day—sophisticated, tolerant, politically aware, and culturally diverse. The church in that city had serious struggles with immorality and "seeker" tolerance, demanding some rather harsh corrections from the apostle Paul. After his first letter to them, Paul wrote again, challenging the Corinthian believers to become aggressively active in spiritual warfare.

Here is God's precise summary of the Church's battle plan against Satan's army:

> For though we walk in the flesh, we do not war according to the flesh. For the weapons of our warfare are not carnal but mighty in God for pulling down strongholds, casting down arguments and every high thing that exalts itself against the knowledge of God, bringing every thought into captivity to the obedience of Christ, and being ready to punish all disobedience when your obedience is fulfilled. (2 Corinthians 10:3-6, NKJV)

This is God's overview of the battle, if you will, and believers—especially church leaders—would do well to examine the specifics of God's instructions to them, broken apart here for clarity:

The major objective is to "pull down strongholds."

- We accomplish this by "casting down arguments."
- We must cast down "exalted ideas" that oppose the knowledge of God.

- We must be ready to "punish disobedience" once our own obedience is complete.

The ultimate objective is to "bring into captivity *every* thought" so that obedience to Jesus Christ is brought about.

Not Individual Warfare

The greatest possible number of troops should be brought into action at the decisive point.
— Karl von Clausewitz

This striking passage cannot be applied to an individual. A "stronghold" is a castle or fortress, a fortified complex that a single warrior would never be able to destroy by himself. An individual, acting alone, cannot pull down a castle or fortress. An individual cannot destroy great plans (military programs, etc.), nor can an individual destroy "every high thing" or "every thought."

This is a job for an army. This is a job for mighty engines of war.

Paul presents a battle plan for the Lord's churches, a responsibility for Christians collectively. The weapons are not the "armour of God" for the individual believer. To pull down strongholds, war engines are needed. Ephesians 6 describes God's provision of spiritual armor each of us should wear as we go into spiritual battle. From an individual perspective, however, the sword of the Spirit and the helmet of salvation wouldn't do much against a castle. A collective might is needed—the collective might and war machines of the Kingdom, and of the Church of which we are all a part.

Age-Long Spiritual Warfare

A certain grasp of military affairs is vital for those in charge of general policy.
— Karl von Clausewitz

The Roman army of the first century used powerful siege engines against the strongholds they conquered. These are what the apostle Paul had in mind as he wrote to the Corinthian church—catapults, battering rams, and ballistae—the kind of major weapons that could take down a fortress.

As always, the word choices of the Holy Spirit are precise. The word translated as "war" in 2 Corinthians 10 is one of only three words in the New Testament used for confrontation.

It is *not* the Greek word *mache*, which is used of individual strife and fights. Note how *mache* is used:

> For indeed, when we came to Macedonia, our bodies had no rest, but we were troubled on every side. Outside were *conflicts*, inside were fears. (2 Corinthians 7:5, NKJV)

> But refuse foolish and ignorant speculations, knowing that they produce *quarrels*. (2 Timothy 2:23, NASB)

> But avoid stupid controversies, genealogies, dissensions, and *quarrels* over the law, for they are unprofitable and futile. (Titus 3:9, RSV)

When God speaks to the issue of conflicts or disputes among believers that produce personal arguments or debates or tensions, He uses the Greek word *mache*.

Neither does God choose the Greek word *polemos* to describe the warfare in 2 Corinthians 10. *Polemos* refers to a major battle (usually a single event), like the "war in heaven."

> And there was *war* in heaven. Michael and his angels fought against the dragon. (Revelation 12:7, NIV)

> And you will hear of *wars* and rumors of *wars*. See that you are not troubled. (Matthew 24:6, NKJV)

> And I saw the beast, the kings of the earth, and their armies, gathered together to *make war* against Him who sat on the horse and against His army. (Revelation 19:19, NKJV)

Polemos is a word for big military events that involve armies. Such a term could be used to define an attack against a "stronghold," but the Holy Spirit chose another.

The word used for "war" in 2 Corinthians 10 is the Greek word *strateuomai*. That word is used specifically for a long-term military campaign. An earthly example would be World War I or II—a multi-year conflict.

In the context of Scripture, it refers to a lifelong or age-long battle. Please note how God uses this word in other passages:

> This charge I commit to you, Timothy, my son, in accordance with the prophetic utterances which pointed to you, that inspired by them you may *wage* the good *warfare*. (1 Timothy 1:18, RSV)

> No one engaged in *warfare* entangles himself with the affairs of this life, that he may please him who enlisted him as a soldier. (2 Timothy 2:4, NKJV)

> Beloved, I urge you as aliens and strangers to abstain from fleshly lusts, which *wage war* against the soul. (1 Peter 2:11, NASB)

When Paul writes about "the weapons of our warfare," he is referring to the lifelong spiritual battle—indeed, the age-long warfare against the great adversary, Satan.

> For though we live in the world we are not carrying on a worldly war, for the weapons of our *warfare* are not worldly but have divine power to destroy strongholds. (2 Corinthians 10:3-4, RSV)

The emphasis is not on an individual "battle" to obtain spiritual victory. Nor is the focus on a gospel witness to "win" a person to Christ. The clear military metaphor is about a major campaign, led by, of course, the "captain of the host of the LORD," the Lord Jesus Christ (Joshua 5:14). The "army" of the Lord is composed of the churches Jesus leads into battle. Keeping with the military imagery, those churches would be organized (by the Lord Jesus Himself) into the spiritual equivalent of divisions, brigades, regiments, battalions, companies, platoons, and squads.

Universal Military Requirements

I had the fortune of serving in the Armed Forces for a number of years, including a deployment to Vietnam, and I well remember the basic requirements of war. Most importantly, when going into battle I must know my opponent. From a personal standpoint, this was often difficult in Vietnam, since the enemy frequently assumed the outward appearance of the general population. The same problem is endemic in today's widespread war against Muslim terrorists.

Perhaps it should not be a surprise, then, that "Satan himself is transformed into an angel of light. Therefore it is no great thing if his ministers also be transformed as the ministers of righteousness" (2 Corinthians 11:14-15). One cannot just assume. We must know who the enemy is.

From a campaign standpoint, however, clear objectives are paramount. What is the campaign about? What are the goals? How do we accomplish them? Then, once the bigger picture is understood, we may begin to set the strategic plans and the tactical logistics necessary to accomplish the larger ends. The strategic plan focuses on the goals of the warfare. The tactics employed and the weapons used flow from the strategic plan as it is implemented throughout the long campaign.

Since the military analogy is so frequently applied in Scripture to the age-long spiritual war, we can learn much about God's charge to His army using the universal military requirements revealed both in Scripture and in history.

Naming the Enemy

In such things as war, the errors which proceed
from a spirit of benevolence are the worst.
— Karl von Clausewitz

No war campaign can ever be successful unless and until the military leadership understands the identity and nature of the enemy. All too often, well-meaning Christian leaders are loath to identify evil—or to recognize that such evil is the constant "roaring" of Satan, "seeking whom he may devour." Some churches are so "seeker driven" that they permit the infiltration of their "army" by agents of the very enemy that they are supposed to oppose.

The Chief Adversary

But while men slept, his *enemy* came and sowed tares among the wheat and went his way....He said to them, 'An enemy has done this.'...The *enemy who sowed them is the devil*, the harvest is the end of the age, and the reapers are the angels. (Matthew 13:25, 28, 39, NKJV)

Be sober, be vigilant; because your *adversary the devil*, as a roaring lion, walketh about, seeking whom he may devour. (1 Peter 5:8)

The chief adversary in our spiritual warfare is Lucifer—identified variously as Satan, the devil, the evil one, the enemy, and simply, "the adversary." Most Christians will never deal with him personally, since they are not usually involved at that level of the strategic battle, but he nonetheless remains in control of his evil forces at his campaign headquarters.

All Christians, however, are involved in this intense spiritual warfare and we will no doubt encounter Lucifer's "army" of spiritual demons—those fallen angels who chose to follow Satan's rebellion against the Creator.

For we do not wrestle against flesh and blood, but against *principalities,* against *powers,* against the *rulers of the darkness* of this age, against *spiritual hosts of wickedness* in the heavenly places. (Ephesians 6:12, NKJV)

These are our enemies. The chief adversary is Lucifer, and it is against that evil archangel and his minions that we fight. We must never lose sight of the "war" that we are fighting, nor the intense hostility of the enemies that we face. Satan is after the destruction of God's people.

The World's Philosophy

The Bible clearly teaches that there is a philosophy behind Lucifer's campaign strategy. It is referred to loosely sometimes as a worldly philosophy—a love of the world's wisdom.

See to it that no one takes you *captive through philosophy* and empty deception, according to *the tradition of men*, according to *the elementary principles of the world*, rather than according to Christ. (Colossians 2:8, NASB)

Do you not know that *friendship with the world is enmity with God?* Whoever therefore wants to be a friend of the world makes himself an enemy of God. (James 4:4, NKJV)

For many walk, of whom I have told you often, and now tell you even weeping, that they are the *enemies of the cross of Christ*: whose end is destruction, whose god is their belly, and whose glory is in their shame—*who set their mind on earthly things.* (Philippians 3:18-19, NKJV)

Because *the carnal mind is enmity against God*; for it is not subject to the law of God, nor indeed can be. (Romans 8:7, NKJV)

This love of the world's way of thinking, embracing of the world's way of doing things, not only dilutes our ability to think clearly as a "soldier" belonging to the Lord's army, but will, if not avoided and resisted, cause us to betray the very One whom we are called to serve. It is entirely possible for a Christian to have his mind "corrupted" (2 Corinthians 11:3), his faith "shipwrecked" (1 Timothy 1:19), to fall from his "steadfastness" (2 Peter 3:17), and to become so "entangled" in the world's philosophy that he is "overcome" (2 Peter 2:20) by the very enemy that he is supposed to be fighting.

It is vital that we stay alert to the dangers of the world's philosophy, by which we learn to recognize our adversary.

The Evil Leaders

There are human agents who have become so dominated by sin and have so yielded themselves to Satan's power that they have become part of our earthly battle. These evil leaders are major officers in the enemy camp who will demand our focused opposition.

The apostle Paul called Elymas the sorcerer "you son of the devil, you enemy of all righteousness" (Acts 13:10, NKJV). He also identified Hymenaeus and Philetus as ones who had "strayed concerning the truth" and were responsible for overthrowing the faith of others (2 Timothy 2:17-18, NKJV). The Ephesian coppersmith, Alexander, was listed by Paul as one of his main adversaries who had "greatly withstood" Paul's ministry (2 Timothy 4:14-15).

The Lord Jesus often confronted the religious leaders in first-century Israel. The words He used to describe their character were not at all complimentary. "Vipers," Jesus called the Pharisees (Matthew 12:34), along with "whited sepulchers…full of dead men's bones" (Matthew 23:27). In fact, Jesus said of those religious leaders that they were of "your father the devil" (John 8:44)! These public rebukes are hardly "politically correct" or tolerant of "alternative views."

While it is clear that Lucifer is the chief adversary in this long spiritual war, there are those among us who accept and promote his teaching and his philosophies. As we seek to identify the enemy, we need to recognize the human leaders who embrace the philosophical systems that empower the deception that is part of the larger spiritual war, and who use them to further the battle.

Understanding the Objectives

This seems so obvious that it could be considered superfluous information. However, one of the more common mistakes in warfare (let alone in business or in personal planning) is to assume that the major objectives (goals) are well known. Many times the ultimate objective is lost among the factions and personal agendas of the leadership. Although this should surely not be the case among the leaders of the Lord's Kingdom, all too often the "General Orders" to the Church are either misunderstood or set aside in favor of "practical" considerations.

Please be reminded of these very clear objectives from our Commander.

Absolute Victory

> *The bloody solution of the crisis, the effort for the destruction*
> *of the enemy's forces, is the first-born son of war.*
> — Karl von Clausewitz

One major spiritual objective should be a focus on absolute victory. Why? Because absolute victory is the stated objective of the Lord Jesus.

Earth history is not a good teacher in this regard. Although there have been a few military campaigns over the centuries conducted with absolute victory in mind (Alexander the Great, Hitler, etc.), most of the regional conflicts in recent generations have had more nebulous ends in mind, such as peace, or some hybrid political settlement, or, more practically, control of economic assets. In spiritual warfare, however, the objective is to obliterate the enemy—absolute total victory, total recognition of Christ as King, total punishment for those who reject Christ, total elimination of all enemies.

Perhaps it would be helpful to review the biblical principles.

Total Recognition of Christ as King

Therefore God also has highly exalted Him and given Him the name which is above every name, that *at the name of Jesus every knee should bow*, of those in heaven, and of those on earth, and of those under the earth, and that *every tongue should confess that Jesus Christ is Lord*, to the glory of God the Father. (Philippians 2:9-11, NKJV)

Total Punishment for All Who Reject Christ

For if *God spared not the angels that sinned, but cast them down to hell*, and delivered them into chains of darkness, to be reserved unto judgment; and spared not the old world, but saved Noah the eighth person, a preacher of righteousness, *bringing in the flood upon the world of the ungodly*; and turning the cities of *Sodom and Gomorrah into ashes* condemned them with an overthrow, *making them an ensample unto those that after should live ungodly*…and to reserve the unjust unto the day of judgment to be punished. (2 Peter 2:4-9)

And then *the lawless one* will be revealed, whom *the Lord will consume* with the breath of His mouth and *destroy* with the brightness of His coming. The coming of the lawless one is according to the working of Satan…among those who perish, because they did not receive the love of the truth…that they *all may be condemned* who did not believe the truth but had pleasure in unrighteousness. (2 Thessalonians 2:8-12, NKJV)

Total Elimination of all Enemies

> *The enemy advances, we retreat. The enemy camps, we harass.*
> *The enemy tires, we attack. The enemy retreats, we pursue.*[2]

But bring here *those enemies of mine*, who did not want me to reign over them, and *slay them before me*. (Luke 19:27, NKJV)

But the cowardly, unbelieving, abominable, murderers, sexually immoral, sorcerers, idolaters, and all liars shall *have their part in the lake which burns with fire and brimstone*, which is the second death. (Revelation 21:8, NKJV)

Fire came down from God out of heaven, and devoured them. And *the devil* that deceived them *was cast into the lake of fire and brimstone*, where the *beast and the false prophet* are, and shall be tormented day and night for ever and ever....And I saw the *dead, small and great*, stand before God...and the sea gave up the dead which were in it; and death and hell delivered up the dead which were in them: and they were judged every man according to their work. And *death and hell were cast into the lake of fire*. This is the second death. (Revelation 20:9-14)

These are important elements to understand. Spiritual warfare is not a political effort. It is warfare for the purpose of annihilation. From a spiritual perspective, Jesus Christ doesn't take prisoners. He either brings about the "new birth" that creates an eternal child of God, or He will judge those worthy of the "second death" (Revelation 21:8). These two goals are vital to absolute victory.

The concept of absolute victory—and the attendant eternal condemnation of those who do not embrace Jesus Christ as King—runs counter to the view many Christians have of God. God is love, is He not? Surely God will overlook the ignorance of "the heathen" or "find a way" to save everyone. But the one attribute that overrides all other divine attributes is God's *holiness*. His love is subject to His holiness. His justice and His mercy are subject to His holiness. Those who ultimately reject everything that Christ stands for will be rejected and cast into an eternity of punish-

---

2   Mao Tse-tung, 1965, A Single Spark Can Start a Prairie Fire, *Selected Works*, Vol. I, Eng. ed., Peking: FLP, 124.

ment. Scripture is clear on this point, from Genesis to Revelation.

Absolute victory demands recognition of Christ as King, punishment for those who reject Him, and the elimination of all His enemies.

Capture the Thoughts

The Bible insists that our battle is an intellectual one. Our weapons are not fleshly. We don't have a literal sword, but we do have a spiritual sword, which is the Word of God. The battle plan is to capture the thinking processes that are exploited by the enemy. This is a vital concept.

The "Law of Sin" in the Flesh Must Be "Captured"

But I see another law in my members, warring against the law of my mind, and bringing me into captivity to the law of sin which is in my members. (Romans 7:23)

The "Natural Brute Beast" Must Be "Destroyed"

But these, as natural brute beasts, made to be taken and destroyed, speak evil of the things that they understand not; and shall utterly perish in their own corruption. (2 Peter 2:12)

But the natural man does not receive the things of the Spirit of God, for they are foolishness to him; nor can he know them, because they are spiritually discerned. (1 Corinthians 2:14, NKJV)

From a spiritual perspective, those who are "dead in trespasses and sins" (Ephesians 2:1) are like "natural brute beasts." As such, they cannot be trained to be good any more than they can "receive the things of the Spirit of God." The ultimate end of that condition is "destruction." The only way to prevent such a horrific end is for the "brute beast" to be "quickened" by "the gift of God...created in Christ Jesus unto good works, which God hath before ordained that we should walk in them" (Ephesians 2:8-10).

Therefore, part of the eternal battle plan is to capture the thinking process, which can only be accomplished through spiritual warfare. It cannot done through fleshly efforts.

Worldly Philosophy Brings Enslavement

As discussed earlier, worldly philosophy brings enslavement to Satan's strategies. The love of worldly wisdom, the empty deception it brings, the adherence to the basic worldly principles, are the pursuits that injure and deceive, that even hijack the thinking process.

> While they promise them liberty, they themselves are slaves of corruption; for by *whom a person is overcome, by him also he is brought into bondage.* (2 Peter 2:19, NKJV)

> ...while we were children, were held in *bondage under the elemental things of the world.* (Galatians 4:3, NASB)

Worldly Wisdom Is Foolishness to God

> For it is written, "I WILL DESTROY THE WISDOM OF THE WISE, AND THE CLEVERNESS OF THE CLEVER I WILL SET ASIDE."...*Has not God made foolish the wisdom of the world?* (1 Corinthians 1:19-20, NASB)

Worldly Traditions and Basic Principles Will Bring Disaster

> ...thus *invalidating the word of God by your tradition* which you have handed down. (Mark 7:13, NASB)

> You therefore...*be on your guard* so that you are not carried away by the error of unprincipled men and *fall from your own steadfastness.* (2 Peter 3:17, NASB)

Promote Obedience

One of the jobs of the church is to teach and train. Our Lord insisted that we "make disciples"—believers who are learning, growing, and maturing.

Yes, the church must be involved in evangelism, bringing people into the Kingdom. But the Bible calls these new converts "babes." Once they have entered the church as infants, they must be brought up in the nurture and admonition of the Lord. We can see this parallel in our families, where parents are responsible to lead their children into wisdom and maturity.

It's not enough just to bring people into the Kingdom. The long-term objective for the church is to bring them into *obedience*. They cannot be brought into obedience, obviously, until they are born again, but being born again should be viewed as only the beginning—not the end goal.

The church also has the task of training its people to take their places as warriors in the battle. They must become growing, maturing adults in God's army, and part of that is learning the obedience, learning the processes, learning how to stand and defend, and learning to be a solution rather than a problem.

Many years ago, when I was being trained to go into Vietnam, I spent time in military classes learning some of the techniques of guerilla warfare. One rather surprising tactic (at least to me) was that we were not always to shoot to kill, but rather to aim for a non-lethal part of the body. The intent was to injure, to inflict severe pain. If you hurt an enemy soldier badly, his screams would draw his fellow soldiers to come to help him. Thus, you will effectively take more combatants out of the battle if you just wound someone than if the soldier is simply killed.

Think about that in terms of spiritual warfare. If churches contain a bunch of screaming, crying, spiritual babies who are constantly demanding help for their "wounds," what does that do to the effectiveness of the Church? Obedience is a result of the heart changing, but it also makes us more mature and more able to do that which God intends. It involves more than obedience—it empowers the righteousness that makes us more effective warriors.

There are three key passages that may help us see the need for this objective.

Obedience to Christ Prevents Judgment

...in flaming fire taking vengeance on those who do not know God, and on those who do not obey the gospel of our Lord Jesus Christ. (2 Thessalonians 1:8, NKJV)

Obedience to Christ Indicates a Heart Change

For this is the love of God, that we keep his commandments: and his commandments are not grievous. (1 John 5:3)

Obedience to Christ Empowers Righteousness

Therefore do not let sin reign in your mortal body, that you should obey it in its lusts....Do you not know that to whom you present yourselves slaves to obey, you are that one's slaves whom you obey, whether of sin leading to death, or of obedience leading to righteousness? But God be thanked that though you were slaves of sin, yet you obeyed from the heart that form of doctrine to which you were delivered. (Romans 6:12, 16-17, NKJV)

Part of achieving this objective is an understanding of what God intends for us to do. Remember, this is the picture for the churches. Yes, individuals are involved in it and are responsible for knowing these things. But this is the organized structure for the way the churches are supposed to be involved in the plan of God.

Punish Disobedience

Many assume that half efforts can be effective. A small jump is easier than a large one, but no one wishing to cross a wide ditch would cross half of it first.
— Karl von Clausewitz

But churches are not just responsible for promoting obedience. They must also punish disobedience. That is part and parcel of an army's effectiveness. You cannot tolerate disobedience in an army. You either discipline disobedient soldiers and train them back to obedience, or you remove them from the army. That's exactly what we are told to do in Scripture.

Jesus laid out disciplinary steps for dealing with an offending brother. The final step is to bring him before the church, but if he will still not listen, he is to be treated like a pagan (Matthew 18:17). That's pretty severe, but it is part of our effectiveness as warriors in the Lord's army. These are things that we are responsible to do, which is why Paul wrote, "If any man obey not our word by this epistle, note that man, and have no company with him" (2 Thessalonians 3:14).

When we do need to administer such discipline, it should be done in love, with the goal of restoring the person involved. The objective is always to bring erring people back to obedience. But if they will not be brought back, they must be removed from the fighting force.

Punishment Will Be Implemented

For if the word spoken through angels proved unalterable, and every transgression and disobedience received a just penalty, how will we escape if we neglect so great a salvation? (Hebrews 2:2-3, NASB)

For if God did not spare the angels who sinned, but cast them down to hell and delivered them into chains of darkness, to be reserved for judgment. (2 Peter 2:4, NKJV)

Punishment Comes through the Church, Not by Individuals

And if he refuses to hear them, tell it to the church. But if he refuses even to hear the church, let him be to you like a heathen and a tax collector. (Matthew 18:17, NKJV)

And if anyone does not obey our word in this epistle, note that person and do not keep company with him, that he may be ashamed. (2 Thessalonians 3:14, NKJV)

Let's review. We have to know the enemy. We must pursue absolute victory; it is what the Lord intends to accomplish. We have to understand that this is a spiritual and intellectual warfare that requires us to capture the thoughts of those under the enemy's control. We must promote obedience and punish disobedience among the soldiers in our own army. All these objectives will guide our spiritual warfare as we participate in the army of God.

USING SPIRITUAL WEAPONS

Given the same amount of intelligence, timidity will do a thousand times more damage than audacity.
— Karl von Clausewitz

What spiritual weaponry does a church need? When the Scriptures were written, warfare was up close and personal. It didn't involve the push of a button to detonate a bomb miles away, or even the pull of a trigger to send a bullet hundreds of feet. War, for most of earth's history, has meant the foul odors of blood spilled and eviscerated bodies, while screams of the wounded and shouts of the warriors filled the air. Chaos seemed to be the only discernable theme amid the fighting.

Spiritual warfare is not meant to be "nice."

Our Weapons Are Not Fleshly

The Greek word translated "weapons" in most of the passages that deal with spiritual warfare is *hoplon*. It is founded on the term for "useful tools" and is translated "instruments" as well as "weapons." This may seem obvious, but since we fight a spiritual battle, we need to use spiritual weapons. All too often, however, church leaders have resorted to manipulative methodology to achieve "success"—which in turn seems to increase the "casualties" among both the leadership and the body.

> For I know that in me (that is, in my flesh) nothing good dwells. (Romans 7:18, NKJV)

> For we are not contending against flesh and blood, but against the principalities, against the powers, against the world rulers of this present darkness, against the spiritual hosts of wickedness in the heavenly places. (Ephesians 6:12, RSV)

Our Weapons Are Righteousness

The "armor" for our churches is not methodology, it is righteousness! Romans 6:13 commands us not to "yield" (present, display) our "members" (body parts) as "instruments" of unrighteousness—rather present them as instruments of righteousness. But note, the "tool" can be used for good *or* for evil. Romans 13:12 insists that we "put on" (clothe ourselves with) the "armour of light." Second Corinthians 6:4-7 demands that we "approve" (stand with, place together) ourselves as "ministers [servants] of God...by the armour of righteousness on the right hand and on the left."

Our major weaponry is *righteousness*. May I suggest that a group of 200 righteous people constitutes a mighty army? One such person is a tremendous light (and we are told to be salt and light in the world), but a righteous church full of righteous people is a powerful, powerful weapon.

Herein is the source of the hatred shown by atheists toward Christianity. Righteousness opposes their sin. When you dig down into the literature of the evolutionists and the proponents of all the worldly philosophies, at the bottom of it is their spoken or unspoken declaration, "We don't want God to rule over us. We want to be able to do our own thing. We like our sin."

When the church displays the armor of righteousness, it is set apart from the world. Sadly, many of our churches look just like the world. Nice, ethical—even moral people are in the local country club. Main Street still has a majority of "good" folks walking around. The church must be *righteous*. It ought to look different, sound different, and be different from the country club or Main Street. We must become convicted about how important observable holiness really is.

Most Christians recognize that individual believers should refrain from adopting the world's "look" or "lifestyle." In fact, it is interesting to note how quickly the secular and anti-Christian pundits will gleefully splash the ungodly behavior of "Christians" through the information media. *They* know that Christians are held to a higher standard.

Yes, we have to earn a living, live in houses, buy "things," and enjoy times of recreation—just like others. But if no one knows that you love the Lord at your workplace, or your home cannot be easily identified by your neighbors as a godly home, or the time spent at the ballpark or the lake or the mountains takes precedent over fellowship with your church—even if your clothes emulate those of the ungodly—you are not letting "your light so shine before men, that they may see your good works, and glorify your Father which is in heaven" (Matthew 5:16).

Similarly, if an unbeliever comes into your church and cannot tell the difference between what is seen and heard in your church and what is seen and heard in worldly venues, your church is sending the wrong message.

Our Weapons Are "Mighty through God"

> For this cause we also, since the day we heard it, do not cease to pray for you, and to desire that ye might be *filled with the knowledge of his will* in all wisdom and spiritual understanding; That ye *might walk worthy* of the Lord unto all pleasing, being fruitful in every good work, and increasing in the knowledge of God; *Strengthened with all might, according to his glorious power,* unto all patience and longsuffering with joyfulness. (Colossians 1:9-11)

The battle plan presented in 2 Corinthians 10:4 encompasses much more than an individual Christian or an individual church. Obviously, our Lord Jesus is conducting an age-long war against the chief adversary, and our part in this conflict is visible only in our segment of time and in our portion of the planet. Were it not for God's "might" so succinctly promised in that little phrase "our weapons are mighty," we would never have the courage to stand against the ungodly.

Jesus said, "With God all things are possible" (Matthew 19:26). The greater our awareness is of the importance, the wonder, and the awesomeness of God's power, the more confident our own spiritual strength will be. Salvation is a work of creation. God has made us a new "creation" (2 Corinthians 5:17) that "is created in righteousness and true holiness" (Ephesians 4:24). We now are equipped and have the effective power with which God raised Jesus from the dead (Ephesians 1:19-20).

These are not minor promises! We are empowered by God to do His work—but we must use *His* might, not ours.

In a world that is going to hell, we are supposed to be part of the solution. We are to approve ourselves by the armor of righteousness (2 Corinthians 6:4, 7). Yes, we have individual armor (Ephesians 6). We have a helmet and a breastplate, a sword belt, a sword, shoes, shin guards, because a soldier must be armed. But in Kingdom battles against the wicked one, we are *part* of the army, not *the* army. How do we fight this battle? Our bodies are to be instruments. We are to use the armor of light. We are to use righteousness.

STRATEGIC PLAN

After we have thought out everything carefully in advance and have sought and found without prejudice the most plausible plan, we must not be ready to abandon it at the slightest provocation. Should this certainty be lacking, we must tell ourselves that nothing is accomplished in warfare without daring; that the nature of war certainly does not let us see at all times where we are going; that what is probable will always be probable though at the moment it may not seem so; and finally, that we cannot be readily ruined by a single error, if we have made reasonable preparations.
— Karl von Clausewitz

Once the goals and overall conditions are clear, a strategic plan must be put into place to implement God's warfare. Tactical decisions come out of the strategic plan. Operational decisions for today, or ten years from now, emanate from the strategic plan. The strategic plan uses the big picture to determine how to fight the battles.

Our strategic plan is contained in 2 Corinthians 10:4-5. It is composed of three major attack elements:

- Pull down the strongholds.
- Cast down the plans to thwart God's message.
- Bring into captivity every thought.

These activities are major efforts and will require "specialists" to accomplish them properly. It is certainly appropriate for us to examine each element carefully.

Pull Down the Strongholds

Keep the forces concentrated in an overpowering mass. The fundamental idea. Always to be aimed at before all and as far as possible.
—Karl von Clausewitz

The Objective Is to "Destroy"—Not Accommodate or Tolerate

The word translated "pull down" is *kayairesiv*, which means to demolish or to extinguish. Perhaps you will recall that one of the key elements of God's battle requirements was total victory. This particular part of the strategic plan demands destruction of the "strongholds" of the enemy. We are to breach the walls of the "castle" of enemy wickedness and evil strength and capture the enemy.

When Roman armies attacked a city, they leveled it. When Titus conquered Jerusalem in 70 A.D. during the Jewish rebellion, he reduced the entire city to rubble—including the Temple, thus fulfilling Jesus' prophecy (Matthew 24:2). That idea of total destruction is in view here.

The church's job is to tear down these great strongholds, these castles of the enemy. We're not to leave them in place out of a misplaced concern for the people inside.

> Thus saith the Lord GOD; I will also *destroy the idols*, and I will cause their images to cease…and I *will put a fear* in the land of Egypt. (Ezekiel 30:13)

> I will overthrow the throne of kingdoms; I will *destroy the strength* of the Gentile kingdoms. I will *overthrow the chariots* and those who ride in them; the *horses and their riders shall come down*, every one by the sword of his brother. (Haggai 2:22, NKJV)

The Old Testament is often accused of being "bloody" and "insensitive" to the needs of people. God's righteous and holy anger was more visible, perhaps, in those times, but the God of the Old Testament is the same God who has issued the order: Pull down the strongholds. From heaven's perspective, Satan and his followers are the enemies of all that is holy and godly. If their "thoughts" cannot be made captive, then destruction is the only possible outcome.

There Are Many "Castles" of the Enemy

The word used in 2 Corinthians 10:4 is *ocurwma* and is only used this one time in the New Testament. The obvious reference is to a "fortress" or "castle" of wicked ideas or behavior.

The secular Greek writers used the term that way. We also find it used in the Septuagint translation of the Old Testament, but since the only time it appears in the New Testament is in this passage, a prominent emphasis is implied. The usage refers to the places where the enemy, Lucifer and his minions, have their strongest empowerment, their biggest defenses.

Jesus used the same imagery when he spoke of the "gates of hell" not being able to "prevail" against the onslaught of the church that He was going to build (Matthew 16:18). The imagery of the "gate" does not picture a moveable object. The gate is purely a "defensive" device, and the power behind the gate is "hell" and its master (Revelation 6:8; 20:14). The "attack" is initiated by the Lord's church in order to "capture" the castle of hell.

Please notice that the word "strongholds" is plural. There is not just one castle. There is not just a single battle that one can finish and then sit back and rest. As long as you are alive, the battles will not end. Until the Lord Jesus Himself returns in power, we will be involved in an age-long warfare.

This is a spiritual warfare, and we are to take the attack to the enemy.

Our Churches Are Thus Empowered and Commissioned

We are empowered by the Holy Spirit of God to do this. You and I together are part of a local church that has the responsibility to be on the attack. Of course, this includes the gospel message. That message contains "the power of God unto salvation" (Romans 1:16). Evangelizing the lost people amounts to "recruiting" soldiers who can then be trained for the war. The ongoing job is training, teaching, and honing the abilities and gifts of the saints to be used offensively against "every thought" that opposes truth.

The Attack Is to Use "the Faith"

The apostle Jude, after beginning to write a history of the "common salvation," was moved by the Holy Spirit to charge us to "earnestly contend for the faith which was once delivered unto the saints" (Jude 3). We are also told that when we "resist the devil" he will "flee from us" (James 4:7). That resisting (to oppose, withstand) is to be "in the faith" (1 Peter 5:9).

Whenever one finds a repeated term or phrase in Scripture, it should be a strong signal that the concept is important to understand. In this case, the phrase "the faith" (using the definite article) appears over 40 times in the New Testament. Each time it focuses on the use of biblical teaching, that body of "scripture" that was "breathed out" by the Holy Spirit.

Jesus Himself provides an excellent example of resisting Satan in "the faith." After He had spent 40 days fasting and praying in the wilderness prior to His public ministry, the enemy came to test Him three times. There in the desert while the humanity of our Lord was at its weakest, the devil sought to draw Jesus away from eternal realities and focus on immediate gratification for food, personal recognition, and unlimited power. In response to each test, and to combat each temptation, Jesus quoted the Word of God.

The power to "resist" is rooted in our knowledge of "the faith." Thus, the battle requires that we have a working knowledge of what the Bible teaches. Peter insists that we should be "ready always to give an answer [an apologetic, defense] to every man" (1 Peter 3:15). Paul notes that we should know how we "ought to answer every man" (Colossians 4:6). The instructions to the apostles, prophets, evangelists, pastors, and teachers in Ephesians 4 were to bring about:

> ...unity of the faith, and of the knowledge of the Son of God, unto a perfect man, unto the measure of the stature of the fulness of Christ: That we henceforth be no more children, tossed to and fro, and carried about with every wind of doctrine, by the sleight of men, and cunning craftiness, whereby they lie in wait to deceive; But speaking the truth in love, may grow up into him in all things, which is the head, even Christ: From whom the whole body fitly joined together and compacted by that which every joint supplieth, according to the effectual working in the measure of every part, maketh increase of the body unto the edifying of itself in love. (Ephesians 4:13-16)

It is a terrible weakness in the Church today that most Christians don't know much about the Bible.

Cast Down Imaginations

Once again the objective is to "destroy" these imaginations. The word translated "imaginations" is *logismov* and is used only two times in the New Testament—here and in Romans 2:15, where it is translated "thoughts" in most versions. These are intellectual imaginations of men who think to do away with God. Much of what makes the "castles" strong are the great plans, the huge ideas, the big concepts of those who "do not like to retain God in their knowledge" (Romans1:28).

The Battle Is Intellectual

In 2009, the world celebrated Charles Darwin's two-hundredth birthday. His book *Origin of Species* has been out since 1859 and still dominates scientific and secular thinking. Although the information in the book is weak and logically fallacious, it has gained credence in the scientific and intellectual worlds—primarily because it provides a way to "think" about our world without God.

This is a different problem than the "strongholds" we are commissioned to "destroy." We might visualize these "imaginations" as the academic confidence of the world. Most academic institutions, including many of those with a Christian heritage, are not focused on the truth of the Scriptures. They embrace or tolerate an atheistic, anti-God philosophy that excludes the Creator from their thinking.

The Objective Is to "Destroy" the "Ideas" against Truth

This is a very real and serious threat. Paul issued several warnings for Christians to guard their minds.

O Timothy, keep that which is committed to thy trust, avoiding profane and vain babblings, and oppositions of science falsely so called. (1 Timothy 6:20)

But I fear, lest somehow, as the serpent deceived Eve by his craftiness, so your minds may be corrupted from the simplicity that is in Christ. (2 Corinthians 11:3, NKJV)

Beware lest any man spoil you through philosophy and vain deceit, after the tradition of men, after the rudiments of the world, and not after Christ. (Colossians 2:8)

These are stern words, but we are in a real battle of total warfare, intent on total victory. You can't compromise. You can't reach political deals with the devil. Our objective is to destroy these ideas that are against the truth.

The word "imaginations" conveys the idea of logistical systems, things that are thought through and from which conclusions are drawn. If A is true, then B must be true. Then, if B is true, C must be true, and so on—a series of reasoning that starts from some common observation and draws conclusions that may well be irrelevant when isolated by themselves. If such reasoning starts with a half-truth or a non-truth, all the conclusions will be corrupted—and corrupting.

The role of the Church in this case is to become aware of such false reasonings and destroy them—casting down everything that exalts itself against the knowledge of God.

Eliminate Every "Lofty Thing" against "the Knowledge of God"

> …destroying speculations and every lofty thing raised up against the knowledge of God. (2 Corinthians 10:5, NASB)

These final descriptions of the "targets" within the Strategic Plan are designed on the one hand to help us see the huge invasion of wickedness in our society, and on the other hand to keep us focused on the real problem—that which seeks to oppose God's revelation.

Here are a few biblical examples of the types of "lofty things" we might encounter.

Population Groups (Matthew 11:23)

Capernaum and Sodom and Gomorrah are examples of concentrations of people who have embraced a lifestyle and a mindset that affect their entire area. The emphasis is on social mores and widespread endorsement of evil. You will recall that Sodom and Gomorrah were destroyed for their sensual evil (primarily for their homosexual decadence). Capernaum was judged for its rejection of doctrinal truth.

Surely it does not take much effort to identify areas in our country, or in our world, that are steeped in evil and anti-God activity. Perhaps even more easily marked are the strident voices of minority views that are twisting the truth of God into "political tolerance" and dragging many into the mouth of hell as they rush into further rebellion and wickedness.

The Church of the Lord Jesus Christ MUST oppose this!

Arrogant Individuals (Luke 14:11)

The wicked walk on every side, when the vilest men are exalted. (Psalm 12:8)

He who says to the wicked, "You are righteous," him the people will curse; Nations will abhor him. (Proverbs 24:24, NKJV)

When the righteous are in authority, the people rejoice; But when a wicked man rules, the people groan. (Proverbs 29:2, NKJV)

There will be some wicked men and women, who are naturally or socially gifted with leadership abilities, who will set themselves up as "authorities" in matters of human behavior. Some will be very subtle and may well be exceedingly popular. Others will influence certain segments of society and may only be significant within certain groups. However and whoever these may be, they can be identified "by their fruits" (Matthew 7:16, 20)

Once again, the responsibility of the church—especially church leadership—is to recognize who they are, understand the dangers of their teachings, and warn the "soldiers" of the horrible potential of their influence.

Against the Knowledge of God

There is an important choice of words in this qualifying phrase. "Knowledge" is the Greek word *gno'-sis*, which denotes academic knowledge, the apprehension of truths—*not* the agreement with truth.

…when *they knew God*, they glorified him not as God, neither were thankful; but became vain in *their imaginations*, and their foolish heart was darkened. *Professing themselves to be wise*, they became fools, and…*changed the truth of God into a lie*, and worshipped and served the creature more than the Creator. (Romans 1:21-25)

The key focus is that these "lofty" things are set "against" God.

For behold, Your *enemies* make a tumult; and those who hate You have *lifted up their head*. They have taken crafty counsel against Your people, And *consulted together against* Your sheltered ones…. For they have consulted together with one consent; They *form a confederacy against You*. (Psalm 83:2-5, NKJV)

One of the reasons why God insists that believers not forsake the assembling of themselves together (Hebrews 10:25) is because we need to constantly be confronted with the Word of God. We also need to assemble together to sing praises to our King. We *need* to do these things! They are part and parcel of an *esprit de corps*. That is an important military concept. That's what the marches are for, and the drums are for, and the 21-gun salutes are for. Those are the things that bind a unit together, that make it feel part of something bigger than it can ever be by itself.

That's why we are supposed to be in the assembly, because we *are* part of something bigger. We are part of the Lord's army—part of that which is good and godly and noble and virtuous and praiseworthy. And while God withholds His judgment, giving men time to repent, we who are part of His army must do His work on earth while He has given us time to do it.

OUR LORD'S EXPECTATION FOR HIS CHURCHES

How do we approach this age-long spiritual war?

1. Know the Enemy
   a. The chief adversary is Lucifer and his minions.
   b. The world's philosophy is the enemy's propaganda.
   c. The evil leaders must be recognized and understood.

2. Focus on the Strategic Plan
   a. Use spiritual weapons.
   b. Pull down the strongholds.
   c. Throw down speculative reasoning.

    d.   Cast down proud and lofty opposition.

3. Recognize the Campaign Objectives
    a.   Absolute victory is expected and promised.
    b.   Capturing thoughts is the end goal.
    c.   Promoting obedience to the laws of Christ is demanded.
    d.   Punishing disobedience is expected.

That's what our churches are supposed to be doing. If that's not going on in your church, try to bring about correction. If you can't, find a church that is. Be a part of the solution. Be a part of that which honors the One who rescued you from sin and death.

Martin Luther has been quoted as saying:

> If I profess with the loudest voice and clearest exposition every portion of the truth of God except precisely that little point which the world and the devil are at that moment attacking, I am not confessing Christ, however boldly I may be professing Christ. Where the battles rages, there the loyalty of the soldier is proved, and to be steady on all the battlefield besides is mere flight and disgrace if he flinches at that point.

In fact, when we run away from where the battle is raging or fail to engage the enemy, no matter how loudly we protest our loyalty, we have deserted our posts and disobeyed our Commander, the Lord Jesus Christ.

IMPORTANT BATTLE ISSUES

> *We must, therefore, be confident that the general measures we have adopted will produce the results we expect. Most important in this connection is the trust which we must have in our lieutenants.*
> — Karl von Clausewitz

From a military perspective, the quickest way to end your career as a soldier is to lose confidence in the commander and his staff. Understanding the strategic plan is absolutely necessary, of course, but intellectual knowledge of the plans will do very little if there is no faith in the leadership. That principle obviously applies to our faith in the Lord Jesus and the authority of the Bible—but it is also important "down line" to those "that have the rule over you…for they watch for your souls (Hebrews 13:17).

Understanding Faith

Faith is critical for victorious spiritual warfare. Remember the list of faith heroes in the book of Hebrews? Each of those men and women, key leaders and examples for the ages, "obtained a good report" (Hebrews 11:39) because of and by their use of faith in their lives. It becomes important, then, for us to be certain that we understand both what faith is and how to gain the use of faith during our time and amidst our battles.

The clear biblical definition of faith is revealed to us in Hebrews 11:1: "Now faith is the substance of things hoped for, the evidence of things not seen." Two key words here are "substance" and "evidence."

The **substance** of things hoped for is the KJV choice for the Greek word *hupostasis* (under support, standing under), translated "being sure" and "assurance" in other English translations. This surely implies a confidence in the "hoped for" (forward-looking) results of the spiritual battle promised and outlined in the strategic plans of the "Lord of hosts." Biblical faith is the "gift of God" (Ephesians 2:8) that "recruits" us into the Lord's army in the first place. That gift of faith "stands under" the authority and power of the resurrected Christ and His expected victory in the days to come.

Biblical faith also includes **evidence**. This precise Greek word, *elegchos*, speaks of a "proof," a "conviction" of "things not seen"—even while we are in and among our present circumstances. Not only are we "drawn" to God by God's own personal intervention (John 6:44), but before we can appropriate this incalculable gift of faith, we "must believe that he [God] is and that he is a rewarder of them that diligently seek him" (Hebrews 11:6). God's great gift of faith enables us to not look at the "things which are seen, but at the things which are not seen: for the things which are seen are temporal; but the things which are not seen are eternal" (2 Corinthians 4:18).

Faith is not a blind leap of incredulity; it is grounded in evidence and substance.

Understanding the Source of Faith

The Scripture is very clear: faith "comes by" hearing the Word of God (Romans 10:17). This principle is so obvious that we often assume the concept is common knowledge, or we have become so comfortable with the Source that we tend to "interpret" the information to accommodate human knowledge or experience. Either of these tendencies is very dangerous. Neither of these ideas is godly.

These "God-breathed" writings are "profitable" for us as we attempt to follow God's instructions and are obviously given by God so that we may be "thoroughly furnished unto all good works" (2 Timothy 3:16-17). Furthermore, this "knowledge" is designed by our Lord to be the instrument by which His "divine power" would provide "all things that pertain to life and godliness" (2 Peter 1:3).

We neglect or change the Word of God at our peril.

Understanding the Foundation of Faith

Once again, this is so obvious that we often overlook or ignore the facts.

The very first example of faith listed in the famous passage in Hebrews is belief in the *fiat* creation of the universe. We are simply told that "through faith we understand that the worlds were framed [structured or put together] by the word of God, so that things which are seen were not made of things which do appear" (Hebrews 11:3). Two important pieces of "substance" and "evidence" are found in this text: first, the creation of the universe was "by the word of God." The term for "word" is most specific. It is the Greek word *rhema*, always used of the spoken (verbal, audible) word. Ten times in the six days of creation, the text records that "God said" something into existence!

There is a very important piece of information here: "He spake, and it was done; he commanded, and it stood fast" (Psalm 33:9). There is no room in the text of the Bible, the *words* of Scripture (the inspired writings), for "millions of years" that are necessary to "develop" the structure and life on earth. None. Those who attempt to insert this idea into the text do so by "interpreting" the words to suit the evolutionary and atheistic theories that have one major goal—to leave God out of the story.

Secondly, the "things which are seen" (whatever we can observe on our planet and in our universe) "were not made of things which do appear." Simply put, that which we can observe and measure and test in our world is the *result* of omniscient and omnipotent processes to which we have absolutely no access or knowledge. Our finite abilities and knowledge are incapable of identifying the creative powers that God used to "speak" the universe into existence. It is not only foolish to deny God's existence (Psalm 14:1), but it is the height of intellectual arrogance to insist that the "creature" can explain by his "wisdom" what the Creator accomplished (Romans 1:22-25).

Science deals with what we can see and touch and reproduce. Faith takes us beyond that very limited sphere of experience to what we cannot see. Whenever we try to reconstruct or understand processes that we really can't see, we need faith. Again, the Bible's primary example of faith is our trust in God's account of the beginning (no human was here when *that* happened). That kind of faith goes beyond what we can see or prove with scientific testing into the realm of "hope" (the Bible uses that word), which allows us intellectual rest about matters we don't or can't see.

From a biblical standpoint, this is the foundation for all knowledge.

ENTANGLEMENTS

No man that warreth entangleth himself with the affairs of this life; that he may please him who hath chosen him to be a soldier. (2 Timothy 2:4)

Here is a serious question for us to consider. If we can't trust the Bible on things that we can check like science, or history, or archaeology, how can we trust it on things that we can't check, like heaven and hell?

It really doesn't make sense to believe God for our salvation but not believe what He tells us in Genesis. If the biblical record of Genesis is not accurate, if it is in fact a lie, as much of modern science teaches—if God is lying to us in the very first information of Scripture about Himself—that creates enormous problems with the rest of the Bible's teachings. Moreover, if the foundational data is not accurate, then we've got real problems with the gospel message. The "good news" is totally based on the historical fact of the Creator's ability to rescue humanity from the consequences of Genesis 3.

The Genesis Allegory

There can be no question that the Bible teaches that an omnipotent God created the universe by His own authority and power. Some have said that the first verse of the Bible is the first test of faith that God places in front of us. That certainly parallels the emphasis that the "faith chapter" (Hebrews 11) places on the creation account.

The science-oriented society of our day openly questions whether or not the Bible is accurate in what it teaches. More specifically, the naturalistic and atheistic worldview of evolutionary science insists that Genesis is, at best, an allegory *about* creation. Unfortunately, a growing number of Christian leaders embrace this idea and are openly teaching that God used a combination of age-long "natural" and "evolutionary" processes over millions of years, stepping in from time to time to create the next stage of progressive order.

This presents a serious problem. The words of Genesis are not difficult to understand, and they clearly speak of a week-long, recent creation by an omnipotent Creator. If that is true, then whatever we can discover by our scientific efforts should support what the Bible reveals to us. And if that "evidence" and "substance" don't support it, God's Word is not telling the truth. The *facts* should verify the accuracy of Scripture—if the words of the Bible are true.

But, we are told, the words really don't mean what the words ordinarily mean—they mean something else. But when we examine the biblical text, the information is very carefully worded. The grammatical syntax is precise, and obviously written as a historical narrative. Genesis is structured carefully, even down to the verbs and the nouns that are used. Genesis is not a poetic book, like the book of Psalms, or The Song of Solomon, or Job, or Proverbs—or even some of the prophetic messages. In fact, Genesis seems to be written so carefully that it couldn't be taken any other way than as a precise history of "the beginnings."

Interpretive Reconstruction

It is very interesting that the major arguments about the biblical text seem to center around the first eleven chapters of Genesis. Just as the first example of faith centers on the creation account, so most of theology (and geology, for that matter) center on how one views the *words* of the text in Scripture.

If the universe was created recently (as the words of the Bible's text clearly teach), and that first age was destroyed by a year-long watery cataclysm (as the words of the Bible's text clearly teach), then the "scientific" theory of evolutionary progression embraced by the majority is plainly wrong. The biblical account is quite specific. Everything was created by the spoken word of an omnipotent and omniscient Creator. It did not evolve slowly out of natural forces acting on eternally existing matter. The words and the sentence structure could not be clearer. There isn't a hint about incalculable ages of "deep time."

What is one to do if "faith" is placed in evolutionary science? The logical step is to interpret the words of Scripture differently, to change the meanings of terms so that the "message" fits the belief. Thus it follows, for example, that the word "day" must surely mean an indeterminate age of time—since science has "proven" that the earth is immensely old. The various elements of the creation week must obviously overlap considerably, since science has "proven" that evolutionary development progressed in a different order than the Bible seems to indicate. Even though "day" in Genesis chapter one is very carefully defined by a period of light and a period of darkness; even though the Bible overwhelmingly uses "day" to describe a 24-hour cycle of light and dark; even though it seems like God is going out of His way to make sure that He has a specific message that He wants us to understand about the way in which and the time He took to create the universe; even though the Bible is consistent throughout in the use of the term, if one's faith is placed in evolutionary science, one *must* take "day" to mean something else.

And of course the various terms that speak about the global characteristic of Noah's Flood are not to be taken literally. Science has "proven" that the vast sedimentary deposits around the globe took millions of years to develop. The 371 days described so carefully in Genesis are obviously speaking about a local event. Even though the three-chapter account in Genesis six through eight uses the word "all" some 20 times to describe the death of every living thing and specifically said that "all the high hills under the whole heaven were covered" by the waters of the Flood; even though Jesus Himself and the apostle Peter insisted that the account in Genesis was absolutely true; even though the poetic and prophetic references to that great Flood consistently and clearly verify the Genesis record, if one's faith is placed in the evolutionary insistence that no such flood ever happened, the one *must* make the "all" of the Genesis Flood mean something else.

Therefore, if one can legitimately "interpret" the words in the Genesis text to mean something other than what those words clearly mean both in their context and in the rest of Scripture, what is to prevent the indiscriminate "interpretation" of *other* words in Scripture? If "day" can mean "millions of years," then why can't "resurrection" or "salvation" or "eternal life" or "hell" or…whatever, be given meanings that are convenient to the theology or the science of personal preference?

❧❦❧

THE DANGERS OF COMPROMISE

Perhaps a short recap is in order. The purpose of this book is to challenge the Lord's churches to be active in the spiritual warfare against the great enemy, Lucifer. The "marching orders" are to destroy the "strongholds" of that enemy, to abolish every "imagination" that dares to exalt itself against the Creator of the universe, and to capture "every thought" so that obedience to the King of kings is maintained.

Those objectives are to be accomplished through *righteous* lifestyles and *holy* character consistently exemplified by the children of God, assembled in spiritual military units known as "churches," using spiritual "weapons" of warfare that are not "fleshly" but rather "mighty" enough to accomplish what God has ordered us to do. The instructions to carry out these "orders" are undergirded and proven by "faith" that is gifted to all in God's army, through the hearing of God's written Word. Many "great and precious promises" are included in this knowledge, guaranteeing us both victory and a share in the "inheritance incorruptible, and undefiled, and that fadeth not away, reserved in heaven for you who are kept by the power of God through faith"(1 Peter 1:4-5).

Compromise Despises God's Word

As discussed earlier, changing the words of God's Word to suit personal preferences or to accommodate evolutionary science is a dangerous and an ungodly venture. Building various "interpretations" to justify favored theories or promote worldly behavior is opening up oneself to God's holy anger levied in righteous judgment on those who would dare to make God a liar (Proverbs 30:5-6).

The One who "inspired" the text has "magnified thy word above all thy name" (Psalm 138:2). There is no place for human authority to treat the precious, eternal, and living Word of God as a "despised" thing, to change the text to satisfy personal preference. May God have mercy on those who do so!

Compromise Negates God's Power

The Lord Jesus frequently took issue with the religious leaders of His day. Those who had set themselves up as the "teachers" of the Jews had become "scholars" of the many "interpretations" of the Laws of Moses. There are some 613 such laws in the Pentateuch, but by the time Jesus walked among the Jews, those laws had multiplied to the point that they had become "heavy burdens and grievous to be borne" (Matthew 23:4).

Many times our Lord debated these leaders, castigating them on occasion for their foolishness, pleading with them at other times to turn from their awful treatment of the Scriptures, and insisting that they free the people they were leading from the bondage of untruth. On at least one occasion, Jesus pointed out that their misuse of the words of God was nothing more than "making the word of God of none effect through your tradition" (Mark 7:13).

Simply put, distorting the words of God to turn the truth into untruth, is to negate the power that is in God's Word to set men free of sin's enslavement.

Compromise Withdraws God's Blessing

This should be obvious. The theme of blessing for obedience and judgment for disobedience runs throughout the Bible. There is application to nations (Psalm 33:12) and to individuals (Proverbs 16:7). The New Testament epistles are replete with instructions on how to receive God's blessings, as well as many warnings of punishment and disfavor when disobedient.

Less easy to understand, however, may be the more subtle compromise that promotes half-truths, maintains a "form of godliness" (2 Timothy 3:5), and falls into the disgusting "lukewarm" condition of Laodicea (Revelation3:16). Such churches think that they are "rich and increased with goods" and have instead become blind to the awful fact that they are "wretched and miserable, and poor, and blind, and naked" (Revelation 3:17).

Ezekiel speaks to the core of this danger:

Also, thou son of man, the children of thy people still are talking against thee by the walls and in the doors of the houses, and speak one to another, every one to his brother, saying, Come, I pray you, and hear what is the word that cometh forth from the LORD. And they come unto thee as the people cometh, and they sit before thee as my people, and they hear thy words, but they will not do them: for with their mouth they shew much love, but their heart goeth after their covetousness. And, lo, thou art unto them as a very lovely song of one that hath a pleasant voice, and can play well on an instrument: for they hear thy words, but they do them not. (Ezekiel 33:30-32)

A CLOSING PRAYER

Ah, Lord God, Thou who art our heavenly Father and our Creator, accept, we pray Thee, our praise and thanks for the unspeakable gift of eternal life granted through our Redeemer and Savior, the Lord Jesus Christ. We gladly acknowledge Thy sovereignty over us, and long for the day when Thy kingdom is come and Thy will is done in earth as it now is in heaven. Even so come, Lord Jesus.

Oh, Lord of hosts, we feel the burden of the enemy so terribly. The new minds and hearts that Thou hast given us delight in the holiness and righteousness of Thy laws, but our sinful flesh struggles in the battle. Empower us, please, great Captain of this spiritual war, that we may fight that good fight of faith and become a part of the coming victory of the counsel of Thine own will. Make it so, Lord Jesus.

Now, sovereign Head of the body, Thine own great assembly of chosen and called ones, increase our effectiveness among our churches as we seek to obey your command to pull down the strongholds of the enemy. Bring to our memories the truths of Thy Word that we might destroy the imaginations of those who dare to exalt themselves against Thee. Sharpen our spiritual weapons that will enable us to capture the thoughts of men and turn their minds to the glorious gospel. Let it be, Lord Jesus.

These petitions, Lord God, we lay at Thy feet at the throne of Thy grace, and expect Thy blessings in accordance with Thy will. Amen and Amen, our gracious Lord Jesus.

FOR MORE INFORMATION

Sign up for ICR's FREE publications!

Our monthly *Acts & Facts* magazine offers fascinating articles and current information on creation, evolution, and more. Our quarterly *Days of Praise* booklet provides daily devotionals—real biblical "meat"—to strengthen and encourage the Christian witness.

To subscribe, call 800.337.0375 or mail your address information to the address below. Or sign up online at www.icr.org.

Visit ICR online

ICR.org offers a wealth of resources and information on scientific creationism and biblical worldview issues.

✓ Read our daily news postings on today's hottest science topics

✓ Explore the Evidence for Creation

✓ Investigate our graduate and professional education programs

✓ Dive into our archive of 40 years of scientific articles

✓ Listen to current and past radio programs

✓ Order creation science materials online

✓ And more!

For a free Resource Guide, contact:

INSTITUTE
for CREATION
RESEARCH
P. O. Box 59029
Dallas, TX 75229
800.337.0375